SAINT THOMAS AQUINAS

Merry Christmas + God bless you,

Mrs Albrecht

Mrs. Rawls

BOOKS BY MARY FABYAN WINDEATT

A Series of Twenty Books
Stories of the Saints for Young People ages 10 to 100

THE CHILDREN OF FATIMA
And Our Lady's Message to the World

THE CURE OF ARS
The Story of St. John Vianney, Patron Saint of Parish Priests

THE LITTLE FLOWER
The Story of St. Therese of the Child Jesus

PATRON SAINT OF FIRST COMMUNICANTS
The Story of Blessed Imelda Lambertini

THE MIRACULOUS MEDAL
The Story of Our Lady's Appearances to St. Catherine Laboure

SAINT LOUIS DE MONTFORT
The Story of Our Lady's Slave, St. Louis Mary Grignion De Montfort

SAINT THOMAS AQUINAS
The Story of "The Dumb Ox"

SAINT CATHERINE OF SIENA
The Story of the Girl Who Saw Saints in the Sky

SAINT HYACINTH OF POLAND
The Story of the Apostle of the North

SAINT MARTIN DE FORBES
The Story of the Little Doctor of Lima, Peru

SAINT ROSE OF LIMA
The Story of the First Canonized Saint of the Americas

PAULINE JARICOT
Foundress of the Living Rosary & The Society for the Propagation of the Faith

SAINT DOMINIC
Preacher of the Rosary and Founder of the Dominican Order

SAINT PAUL THE APOSTLE
The Story of the Apostle to the Gentiles

SAINT BENEDICT
The Story of the Father of the Western Monks

KING DAVID AND HIS SONGS
A Story of the Psalms

SAINT MARGARET MARY
And the Promises of the Sacred Heart of Jesus

SAINT JOHN MASIAS
Marvelous Dominican Gatekeeper of Lima, Peru

SAINT FRANCIS SOLANO
Wonder-Worker of the New World and Apostle of Argentina and Peru

BLESSED MARIE OF NEW FRANCE
The Story of the First Missionary Sisters in Canada

SAINT THOMAS AQUINAS

The Story of "The Dumb Ox"

By
Mary Fabyan Windeatt

Illustrated by
Sister Mary Jean Dorcy, O.P.

TAN Books
An Imprint of Saint Benedict Press, LLC
Charlotte, North Carolina

Nihil Obstat: Jerome Palmer, O.S.B.
                   Censor Deputatus

Imprimi Potest: ✠ Ignatius Esser, O.S.B.
                   Abbot of St. Meinrad's Abbey

Imprimatur: ✠ Joseph E. Ritter, D.D.
                   Archbishop of Indianapolis
                   Feast of Saint Dominic
                   August 4, 1945

This book first appeared, in serial form, in the pages of *The Torch*. This book was previously published in book form under the title of *My Name Is Thomas*.

ISBN: 978-0-89555-420-8

Library of Congress Catalog Card No.: 92-82033

Printed and bound in the United States of America.

TAN Books
An Imprint of Saint Benedict Press, LLC
Charlotte, North Carolina
2012

for
REV. FRANCIS N. WENDELL, O.P.,
Provincial Director of the Third Order of
Saint Dominic, in grateful appreciation.

CONTENTS

INTRODUCTION

I HAVE been dead a long time. In fact, I died on March 7, 1274, and my body now rests in the Dominican church in Toulouse, France. But my body is the least important part of me. It is my soul that matters, and my soul has been having a wonderful time for hundreds of years because it is in Heaven.

Through the grace and by the gift of God, my soul sees all the boys and girls in the world today. My soul knows each of you very well, the schools you attend, the teachers who instruct you in religion, arithmetic and geography. My soul is very anxious that you do well in school, that you learn much—especially about our holy Catholic Faith, and that you grow up to do great things. This is not so strange, since some years ago the Pope made me Patron of Catholic Schools. He gave me special charge of each Catholic student in the world. I have been very busy since then helping boys and girls in their work.

As I said, my body is in the French city of Toulouse, but my soul is very much alive. Someday your soul and my soul will meet. In the meantime, please believe that I am your friend, always ready to listen to your troubles, your plans, your studies.

But who am I?

SAINT THOMAS AQUINAS

CHAPTER ONE

I GO TO SCHOOL

M Y NAME is Thomas, and I was born in a castle
in Italy in the year 1225. My father was a rich
man, the Count of Aquin, and I was his third son.
Poor Father! He was a good soul and he made great
plans for me. When I was six years old, he sent me
to school at the Benedictine Abbey of Monte Cassino.
He told my teachers I was to be a priest.

"My two oldest boys will be soldiers like myself," he
said. "I think Thomas should go into the service of
the Church."

I went off to school with my future clearly mapped
out for me. I was to be a monk. More than that. My
father said that when I was older I was to be Abbot
of Monte Cassino, a position held for some years by
his own brother. My mother, whose name was Theodora, agreed with him.

"I'm so proud of you, Thomas!" she often said.
"Someday you'll be in charge of that wonderful Abbey.
Everyone will look up to you as long as you live!"

What could I say? I loved my parents and had been
brought up to obey them. When I finally saw my
uncle, the Abbot of Monte Cassino (he was a white-
haired old man in a black robe, with a gold cross
around his neck and a handsome ring on his finger),
I began to wonder. What kind of an Abbot would I
make? My hair was not white. I didn't know how to

1

read. And I had a feeling that I could never spend my whole life in one place, even in such a beautiful place as the Abbey. There were other difficulties, too. Suppose the monks did not want me for their leader when I was grown up? Suppose some other boy would make a better Abbot?

"Don't worry about such things," my father said. "If I wish my son Thomas to be head of the Abbey, he'll be head of it. Never fear. Am I not Count Landulph of Aquin? Am I not a nephew of the great Emperor, Frederick Barbarossa?"

"Yes, Father," I answered meekly. But I had a strange feeling as I said these words. I, Thomas of Aquin, would never be a Benedictine Abbot. Although I was only a six-year-old boy, I felt quite sure that some other kind of life would be mine.

I liked going to school at Monte Cassino, however. The rugged mountain where Saint Benedict and his monks had settled seven hundred years before was really beautiful. The other boys and I often watched the monks laboring in the fields. We went into the work rooms, too, and saw cloth being woven from wool, old manuscripts being copied in the library. Always there was a lot of activity going on at Monte Cassino, for long ago, when Saint Benedict had first founded his colonies of monks, he had insisted upon two things. The monks should work with their hands many hours every day. They should also spend themselves in praising God by the chanting of Psalms and other prayers. Nothing was to be preferred to this latter work.

So it was that Monte Cassino resembled a very busy but a very holy town. The monks grew every-

I was to be a monk, too.

thing that was necessary to feed themselves as well as the boys who studied in their school. Then, at certain hours, they went to their chapel to sing the praises of God. Sometimes, as I listened to these holy men chanting the ancient Psalms, I wondered if it might not be good to spend my life at Monte Cassino.

Everything was so orderly and peaceful.

But as soon as such thoughts came, a strange little voice inside me would start to laugh.

"You're not going to stay here, Thomas. Someone else will be Abbot."

"Why?"

"Because it's God's Will."

"How do you know?"

"I just know. And don't keep asking me questions."

I wondered who was right, my father or the little voice. It seemed as though I would stay forever at the Abbey. But when five years had passed, a great thing happened. I was sent home to Rocca Secca, to the great castle where I had been born. I was eleven years old now, and it was good to see my family once more—Father, Mother, my sisters and brothers. Mother cried a little when she saw me first, but soon she was all smiles.

"Oh, Thomas! How I've missed you! And how big you've grown! Look, Landulph, he's really very tall for eleven!"

My father made funny noises in his throat, but his eyes were kind as he looked me up and down.

"Not bad, not bad at all," he murmured. "The monks seem to have treated you very well."

"Yes, Father. The Abbey is a wonderful place."

"And what have you learned, son?"

"To read and write in Latin. And a little of many other things, Father. When am I going back?"

A peculiar look came over Father's face. "You're not going back, Thomas. Instead you're going to go to school in Naples. At the University."

Naples! The University! I could hardly believe my ears. What had made Father change his mind? Something must be wrong. Perhaps my teachers at Monte Cassino hadn't been pleased with the way I did my lessons.

"Thomas," said Mother very gently, "the monks tell us you're a good student and should have every advantage. They think that in Naples . . ."

"They think you've learned everything they can teach you," my father interrupted. "Ah, lad, we're proud of you! Going to the University at eleven! When you get your degree you'll be the most learned Abbot Monte Cassino ever had!"

So my little voice had been wrong! I was going back to Monte Cassino someday to rule the monks, to live far away from the noise and bustle of towns and cities. But first there was to be a course of studies at the University.

"Son, you look tired," said Mother presently. "We mustn't have that. Why not go to your room for a while?"

I nodded. I was tired. And puzzled, too. It seemed too much to believe that my school days at the Abbey were over. But I could see Father smiling to himself as I left the room. He, at least, was at ease about my future. He looked just the way he did when his soldiers came back from winning an important battle.

My sisters, Marietta and Theodora, were just as

excited as anyone else over the news that I was going
away to the University.

"It must be wonderful to be a boy and go places!"
sighed Marietta. "Thomas, do you suppose we could
go with you to Naples?"

"I'd love living in a big city," put in Theodora wist-
fully. "Mother, could we go with Thomas?"

"Nonsense!" said Mother. "Girls like you have no
reason to live in Naples. You'd just get foolish ideas
there."

Theodora laughed. "Maybe we could find ourselves
husbands," she suggested. "Probably there are many
nice young men in Naples who haven't picked out a
wife yet."

"Thomas will meet lots of them at the University,"
said Marietta. "Oh, it would be just wonderful if we
could go!"

Mother shook her head. "Naples is a wicked city.
Perhaps even Thomas shouldn't be going there,
when he's so young. But as for you two . . ."

The girls stopped their teasing. It was all a joke
anyway, for they were too young to be thinking of
marriage. But their excitement about my leaving
home continued to increase. The whole summer I
was at Rocca Secca they could talk of nothing else.

"You'll study hard and make yourself famous, won't
you?" Marietta asked one night. "Father and Mother
are so proud of you, Thomas. It would break their
hearts if you were lazy."

"Father has always said you would grow up to
be Abbot of Monte Cassino," Theodora added. "You
mustn't disappoint him."

I thought of the little voice that continued to tell

me my life would never be spent at the Abbey, but there was no use in saying anything to the girls. "Of course I'll work hard," I promised. "Never fear. And you be good and see that Father and Mother aren't disappointed in you!"

Marietta and Theodora laughed. "We can't be anything but good in this poky old castle," they said. "You ought to know that, Thomas."

My brothers, Landulph and Raynald (who were much bigger than I and very good at horseback riding and fighting with swords), treated me like one of themselves during the last few weeks I spent at home.

"So our little Thomas is going away to the big city," said Raynald one day. "That's what happens to a boy when he's good at books. Thomas, you're a lucky little beggar to get such a chance!"

"Father never sent us to the University," put in Landulph, pretending to be jealous. "A fine time we might have had there, too."

I could not help smiling. No one hated books and study as much as these two older brothers of mine. Father had trained them to be soldiers. They would have been bored to death at the University. They knew it. And so did I.

Chapter Two
I Go to Naples

DEAR FATHER did not want me to go to the city alone. He hired a tutor, a young man who was to live with me in Naples, help me with my school work and keep me company. We got along very well, the tutor and I, and I was happy as a University student.

Not one of my companions was my age, however. Some of them laughed at first, when they saw an eleven-year-old boy in their classes. But they did not laugh long.

God gives some children the gift of a good voice, an interest in art, ability at games. Certainly He had given my older brothers the gift of physical strength, so that they could use a sword and ride a horse far better than their companions. To Marietta and Theodora He had made the gift of striking personal beauty. But for me there was a far different gift. God had given me a quick mind and a good memory.

Because of this, books were always my special friends. Even at the University there was no branch of study which I found difficult. Mother had once told me that my interest in the printed word showed itself very early. When I was a baby, she said, the only thing that would stop my tears was a piece of paper with writing on it. Once, when I was only a few months old, someone had given me a paper bear-

ing the words of the Hail Mary. When my nurse tried
to take it away, I ate it!

I worked hard at the University and did quite well
in every subject. One of my teachers, a clever Irish-
man named Master Peter, used to take me aside
sometimes for a little talk.

"Thomas, you're very lucky. I don't think I ever
taught a boy with so much sense as you have. What
are you going to do with your life?"

I told Master Peter about Father, and his plans for
having me become a Benedictine monk. I also said
that I found school work easy only because God had
given me a quick mind and a good memory. Apart
from knowing books, I had little claim to fame.

"That's right," said Master Peter. "You're not particularly good-looking. And I notice you're a rather
awkward lad—no good at all at sports."

I smiled. Master Peter was noted for being very
much to the point. "That's right, Master Peter. I'm
not a bit like my brothers."

"Tell me, lad, why you think you've been given a
good mind? You know the gifts God makes are always
for some purpose."

I nodded. My brothers were strong so that they
might be good soldiers and help my father keep
order in the country. My sisters were pretty so that
they might get married and have children. (Of course
there was no reason why they couldn't be nuns,
either. A pretty face with a good heart to keep it company can make a convent a very cheerful place.) But
I? Why had I been given a good mind? Why was all
learning a thing of delight?

"Maybe you're meant to be a teacher," suggested

I worked hard at the University.

Master Peter. "Maybe you can help young people in their school work. Would you like that?"

Would I like it? I told Master Peter I would just love it! But then (and I could not help feeling a little sorry for myself) Father would never hear of such a thing. He didn't want me to spend my life as a teacher. He wanted me to be Abbot of Monte Cassino—to govern hundreds of holy monks in the beautiful Abbey that was only six miles away from home.

Master Peter must have seen how troubled I was, for soon he stopped asking questions about what I expected to do with my life.

"I think that all we can do right now is pray," he said kindly. "God will see that things turn out well for you."

I stayed at the University for seven years, living with my tutor, studying many different subjects, always passing my examinations with honors. I made many friends, particularly among the students who were not clever and who needed help to get along. I was very happy these days, especially when I could give some boy a hand with his work.

"How I envy you!" said a young fellow to me one day. "You remember everything you read. You look through a book once and after that it's in your head. How do you do it, Thomas?"

"God helps me," I said, and explained to my friend that I had been given the ability to learn quickly while other people possessed gifts which I should never have. Then I tried to show the young man that there are all kinds of flowers in the world—red roses, white lilies, blue violets, yellow daisies.

"Which is the most beautiful?" I asked. He looked a

little puzzled. "They're all beautiful, I suppose, only each in a different way."

"Then one isn't better than another?"

"No."

I laughed. "God gave flowers different colors and perfumes. He's given men different talents, too. We don't have to wonder why. All we have to do is use what talents we have in the best possible way."

Naples is a beautiful city. During my seven years' stay there I took many long walks. Often I would meet some of the University students strolling in the streets, or paying a visit to one of the numerous churches. As the years passed, I came to know the city very well. There were two sections. One was made up of fine avenues and beautiful buildings. Here lived those high in society and politics. The other part of Naples was poor. It was hardly safe to go there at night because of the thieves and ruffians who lurked about the dimly lit streets. It was also known to be a place where wicked people lived. These poor souls, the women in particular, made fun of God and His Church. The Sacrament of Matrimony was just a joke to them, likewise the virtue of purity. The women in this part of Naples often tried to make friends with the students from the University.

"Let us show you how to be really happy," they said. "Don't you know it's foolish to be spending all your time with books?"

Many of the students did go down to this part of the city, but they never found happiness there. All they found was sin. It made me very sad when I saw several of my own friends going down to this part of Naples to forget about God and His Commandments.

One day, when I was about fifteen years old, I passed a church which belonged to a new religious Order—the Friars Preachers. The founder of this group of priests and Brothers had been a Spaniard, a wonderful preacher named Dominic de Guzman. When I was a small boy, attending the Abbey school at Monte Cassino, the Pope and his Cardinals had declared Dominic a saint. I had never known much about him, but in the streets of Naples I sometimes came across his followers, men who wore habits of white wool covered with a flowing black cape. They were not very numerous as yet. Neither were the brown-clad friars of Saint Francis of Assisi. But it was well known that the numbers of both religious groups were increasing.

I don't know how it came about, but on one of my visits to the Dominican church I suddenly understood there was no use in Father's expecting me to be a Benedictine monk. I wanted to be a Dominican friar. Nothing else.

"Now you're on the right track," said the little voice inside me. (By now I had come to respect this voice a good deal.) *"The Dominican life is one of preaching and teaching, Thomas. You'd like it very much."*

The Dominican life! So this was why I had never felt suited to being an Abbot. All the time God had meant me to be a friar, a poor servant ever on the move, with no great Abbey for a home but just the crowded towns where one was sent to work.

"You could go and ask to become a Dominican right now," the little voice continued. *"The Father Prior has heard of your good work at the University."*

I felt my heart beating faster. "But my family?

They'll be furious if I become a friar instead of a monk."

"And what if they are?"

"But I don't want to hurt them!"

"You mean you're afraid."

"I'm not afraid. Only Father and Mother will be so disappointed! After all, they've spent a lot of money on my education . . ."

"You are afraid, Thomas. You're a coward."

"I am not!"

Right then and there I refused to argue longer with the little voice. Instead, I hurried to the house where I knew the friars lived. Before five minutes had passed, I was asking to be admitted to the Order of Friars Preachers, which the great Saint Dominic had founded some twenty-five years before.

The Prior was not long in deciding that I was too young to be a friar.

"Fifteen? I'm afraid that won't do, Master Thomas. Even though we are much in need of helpers, you're still just a boy. Come back when you're eighteen years old and perhaps it will be a different story."

"You mean I can be a Dominican in three years?"

"If you'll promise to work hard and pray well in the meantime. The life of a Dominican is not easy, you know. It won't hurt to get ready for it in plenty of time."

I went back to my lodgings, sad and happy by turns. Three years seemed so long! Perhaps I might not even live to see my eighteenth birthday!

But it was not I whom death presently called. It was Father. The good man went home to God in the same year that I finished my studies at the University. His passing made me sad, yet not too much so. Very soon, I told myself, I would be a Dominican friar. After more study, I could hope to be a priest. Once I was a priest, I could offer the Holy Sacrifice for the happy repose of Father's soul. I could be really useful to him, with the help of God's grace.

Sometimes, during those weeks before my entrance into the Dominican Order, I would lie awake at night for hours. Dominicans were men who preached and taught in the great cities, among pagans and sinners. Usually they settled in the neighborhood of schools and Universities, converting students and professors from error. Soon I might be numbered among these same fine men. Soon I might be allowed to use my learning, the good mind God had given me, in the work for which Saint Dominic's sons were fast becoming famous.

But as I pictured myself in the black and white habit of the Order, doing everything to prove my gratitude for such a wonderful vocation, my little voice would start to speak again:

"Yes, you should be glad about being a Dominican, Thomas. On the other hand . . ."

"On the other hand, what?"

"There's going to be a lot of trouble, too."

"Trouble?"

"Loads of trouble. Just wait until your mother hears about your plans! And your brothers! And your sisters! Oh, Thomas, what a fuss there's going to be!"

CHAPTER THREE

I GO TO PRISON

THERE certainly was a fuss when my family learned that I had become a friar at the Dominican convent in Naples. My brothers swore that I had disgraced them. My sisters cried. And Mother? She was the worst of all.

Since Father's death she had become head of the family. Now she declared she was leaving Rocca Secca and coming to Naples to bring me home. If I would not obey, she would go to see the Archbishop of the city. Or the Master General of the Order. Or even the Pope.

"Thomas is going to take off that wretched white habit!" she stormed. "Doesn't he know how his father (Lord rest his soul!) always planned for him to be Abbot at Monte Cassino? Oh, if I could just get my hands on that thoughtless boy!"

The good Prior at Naples was very much worried. "I don't know what we're going to do!" he told the other friars. "The Countess Theodora is already on her way to Naples. They say she is furious, that she will stop at nothing to take Brother Thomas from us! Oh, dear! Nothing like this ever happened to me before!"

I felt sorry for the good Prior, for all the trouble my family was causing, but I knew that nothing could make me change my mind. I had been given the black and white habit of Saint Dominic's sons. I would die rather than give it up.

Before Mother could reach Naples, my superiors ordered me to our convent at Rome. But news of my whereabouts leaked out and presently word had reached the Prior that Mother was on her way to the Eternal City. As it happened, Father John, Master General of the Order, was at Rome just then. He suggested that I accompany him to Paris. Once I was out of Italy, Mother could do little to make me stop being a Dominican.

It seemed a very good idea to the Prior, and soon I packed and was ready to go to Paris.

There were three other friars in the company, besides Father John, and we lost no time in getting under way. My sadness at leaving Italy was lessened somewhat at the thought of the busy life which awaited each of us in Paris. The Dominican Order had a flourishing convent there where classes in University subjects were held. Probably I would soon be a student again.

"You look more cheerful, Brother Thomas," said Father John as we stopped for a rest one afternoon. "Now that we are well out of Rome and the danger of your mother's wrath, we should all feel better."

I nodded. We had successfully covered many miles by now, having reached Aquapendente, near Siena.

"It was a good idea to take me with you to Paris, Father."

But even as I spoke these words, my eyes suddenly caught sight of a little band of horsemen in the distance. Surely it could not be that Mother was trying another plan, that she had sent my soldier brothers to take me prisoner! Yet, as I stared at the riders, more visible now despite the cloud of dust, my heart sank. There was no mistaking the two figures at the head of the little company. Only Landulph and Raynald could ride so recklessly as that.

"Dear God, don't let them take me home!" I prayed. "Let them understand that I want to be a friar more than anything else in the world!"

God had other plans, however. He had sent my brothers after me to see if my new vocation could really stand a test.

Raynald and Landulph lost no time in stating their business. They jumped from their horses, glared angrily at my friar companions, then took me roughly by the arm.

"You're coming home, Thomas. Take off that friar's habit. We've brought you some decent clothes."

I tried to be calm. "My brothers are only joking," I said to Father John. "They don't mean what they say."

"We do mean what we say! Take off that white habit at once. We're taking you home on Mother's orders."

"But I won't go with you! And I won't take off Saint Dominic's habit! What right have you to ask such a thing?"

Then the fight began. Poor Father John, although he was Master General of the Order, could do nothing to help me. Neither could the other three friars. I was knocked to the ground and the habit I loved all but torn from my back.

Raynald and Landulph, growing angrier each minute, finally ordered their soldiers to carry me off by force.

"Take off that white habit!"

"Tie his hands and set him on a horse!" ordered Raynald sharply. "We've had enough nonsense from this foolish boy!"

The next thing I knew I was bound like a criminal, hoisted onto a horse, and on my way to Rocca Secca.

"I'll be back," I managed to call to Father John and the others. "They can't keep me at home forever!" But there were tears in my eyes as I realized the bitter struggle that lay ahead.

It was a tiresome journey home. When the great family castle finally came into view, I shut my eyes wearily. My beloved white habit was torn and dirty, and I could scarcely keep the anger out of my heart. What had I done to be treated so unfairly? Who had a right to keep me from following my vocation?

There was a dreadful scene when Mother and I finally met. Nothing I said could change her heart about the Dominican Order. She considered it a disgrace that certain of the friars begged for food from door to door; that we had no famous Abbey such as Monte Cassino; that we went about preaching to all manner of people.

"Suppose they sent you to beg for food?" she cried. "What would you do?"

"I'd try to beg well, Mother."

That was the wrong thing to say, however, for Mother started to cry as though her heart would break. She could not forget that she was Countess of Aquin, that she was descended from the powerful Norman barons who had conquered Sicily two hundred years before. She really believed I had disgraced our family by becoming a friar.

Finally my brothers spoke up. Since I would not

leave the Dominicans, they said, why not see what a little starvation would do? A taste of solitary life in a prison cell? So presently I was hurried away from Rocca Secca to another castle owned by the family. It was two miles distant and was known as Monte San Giovanni. It was a gloomy place at best, and I did not relish being kept a prisoner there. But what other course was open?

Landulph and Raynald locked me in a damp tower room. I was to stay there, they said, until I came to my senses. From time to time I might speak to Marietta and Theodora. I would be given enough bread and water to sustain life. Other than that, they didn't care what happened. I was a headstrong boy. The seven years at the University of Naples had given me strange ideas. If Father were alive, he would have been thoroughly ashamed of me.

It was very cold and lonely in the tower. When a year had passed, I found Mother still firmly set against my hope of being a Dominican. She very rarely came near me, but Landulph and Raynald appeared from time to time to taunt me for being a fool. Marietta and Theodora also did their best to make me reconsider. Sometimes they brought me a tasty meal, for they were worried about my health. And they smuggled a few books to my tower prison, too. One of these was the Bible.

"Why don't you give in, Thomas?" cried Marietta one day. "You'll die if you stay in this awful old tower much longer."

"Mother is very gloomy," added Theodora. "She really loves you, Thomas, and wants you to be happy. It's her pride that makes her treat you this way. Couldn't you stop being a Dominican, seeing it makes everyone so unhappy?"

As well as I could I tried to explain to the girls what it means to have been given a special work.

"I'm convinced God has given me just one work," I said. "It's the work of studying, and later teaching, as a Dominican friar. If I do this work to the best of my ability; if I don't worry about anything else, I'll save my soul. That's what following a vocation means. It means faithfully traveling the road we know will take us straight to Heaven."

Marietta sighed. "When you speak like this, Thomas, I can't help thinking you're right. If only I could help you in some way! And if only I had some idea as to the road God wishes me to go!"

Now Theodora's eyes were shining. "I feel just the same," she said softly. "And I think you're wonderful to be so brave, to hold out for what you think is right."

It made me feel much better to know that at last my sisters were coming to my side. Before they left I promised to pray that soon each would find the work God wanted her to do. They in turn said they would strive to make life a little more pleasant for me.

As the months passed, I was happy in the thought that perhaps my brothers would have a change of heart, too. Alas, I soon discovered my error. One night, as I sat reading the Bible, there was a sudden knock on the door.

"Come in," I said, thinking it was the old servant bringing me the usual bread and water. But it was not the servant. It was a strange girl. She was older than I, and right away it was clear she was not a

I drew the Sign of the Cross.

good person. She reminded me of the wicked women of Naples, those women who so often tried to tempt young students to do wrong.

"Good evening, Master Thomas."

I looked at this poor creature. Although some would have called her beautiful, I saw only that she had made herself a tool of the Devil, that her soul must be black with sin. Suddenly I was furious at my brothers. Landulph and Raynald had sent this creature to me. They hoped I would fall in love with her, that I would forget about God and the work He wanted me to do in the Dominican Order.

"You'd better go," I said quietly.

"But Master Thomas! I want to make you happy!"

I sprang to my feet. My brothers were soldiers, well used to the ways of the world. They had paid this girl to come and tempt me. They knew how lonely I was, after eighteen months in a miserable tower room. No doubt they thought this would shake my vocation.

There was a fireplace in the corner of the room. I ran toward it, took a smoldering log from the grate and started after my visitor.

"Get out of here!" I cried. "And tell my brothers their miserable trick has failed!"

The poor girl, convinced I was a madman, rushed from the room in terror. When the door had slammed shut, I found myself with the burning brand still in my hands. Trembling, I drew the Sign of the Cross with it on the cold stone wall of the tower.

CHAPTER FOUR

I GO TO COLOGNE

FRESH sorrow was in my heart over the wretched trick my brothers had played. To comfort myself, I knelt down to pray.

"Dear Lord, what am I going to do?" I cried. "Do I have to stay in this tower forever? Don't You really want me to be a Dominican friar?"

Suddenly it seemed as though the tower were warm and bright, that sweet music sounded in my ears, that out of nowhere two shining angels had come to comfort me. In their hands they carried a piece of cord which had fifteen small knots. This they put around my waist. They tied the cord so tight that I cried out with pain. But the angels only smiled and told me there was no reason to be afraid.

"Dear Thomas, God is very greatly pleased with you," they said. "Through His mercy you are to remain pure in body and soul for the rest of your life."

As quickly as they had come, the angels vanished. Soon I fell into a deep sleep. When I awoke, I wondered if the whole thing had not been a dream. But no. There was the cord about my waist, with its fifteen small knots. It could not have been a dream. Something really wonderful had taken place in the tower. At once I promised myself that I would always wear this cord. No one would ever know about it, but it would be there—reminding me of the great miracle of grace which had just been granted to me.

I continued to live in my prison, spending much time with the books my sisters brought me. The Bible was my particular favorite, and I succeeded in memorizing most of it. There was little else to do, it seemed. But there came a day when my sisters rushed into my room with some wonderful news.

"Thomas, you're going to be free at last!" cried Marietta. "The Pope's heard about Mother keeping you here and he says it's a shame!"

"And the Emperor, too!" put in Theodora excitedly. "He's given orders for your release. Oh, Thomas, isn't it wonderful?"

I could hardly believe my ears. Freedom at last! But then a doubt crossed my mind. Was this another trick? Were my sisters deceiving me, as my brothers had tried to do?

"You know there's no use in setting me free if I can't be a Dominican," I said. "That's the only life I want."

Marietta smiled. "You can be a Dominican," she whispered. "Theodora and I are going to see that everything works out just the way you wish."

Then she explained that my family was afraid of the Pope and the Emperor, of what might happen if I were kept a prisoner any longer.

"Landulph and Raynald have promised to look the other way while we help you escape," said Theodora. "Oh, Thomas! Will tonight be all right for you? You won't be afraid if we let you down from the window in a basket?"

Marietta's eyes were shining. "There'll be some Dominican friars waiting for you when it's dark,

Thomas. They'll see that you're taken to a safe place."

I felt like laughing. Although I had read the life of Saint Paul, how he had escaped from prison in a basket, never once had I thought the same thing would happen to me.

"I'll be ready by tonight," I said. "God bless both of you for your kindness."

Several hours later, when darkness had descended upon the world, my sisters brought a large basket to the tower. They also had some strong rope. We fastened both together, tied the rope to an iron ring in the wall, and presently I was being let down from my prison through the narrow window. Far below on the ground, half hidden in the shadows, I could see a little group of friars waiting for me. Up above, their heads outlined against the dim lamplight, Marietta and Theodora let the rope pass slowly through their hands.

"Don't be frightened," they called softly. "We won't let go until you reach the ground."

Slowly, very slowly, I went down the side of the tower in the basket. It was farewell to home. I should have liked to go with Mother's blessing, but it was not to be. For some strange reason, God was arranging things in quite another way.

It was good to be with my Dominican friends again. Shortly after arriving at our convent in Naples, I made my profession as a religious. It was toward the end of January, in the year 1245, and I was twenty years old. A few days after the ceremony, Mother made one last effort to take me away from the Order. She went to Rome and asked the Holy Father, Pope Innocent IV, to set aside my vows.

"Thomas, you're going to be free!"

Wishing to hear my side of the story, the good man ordered me to appear before him in Rome. The trip did not take long and soon I was at the Vatican, explaining to the Pope how much I wanted to be Saint Dominic's son, to pray and teach and write as a simple friar.

"You seem fond of the Dominican habit, Brother Thomas."

"Very fond, Your Holiness. As you know, I've been a prisoner for eighteen months because I refused to give it up."

The Holy Father smiled. "Your good mother wants you to be Abbot of Monte Cassino. How would it be if you went there, assumed the duties of Abbot, yet continued to wear this white habit which you admire so much?"

I was puzzled. How could I be a Benedictine Abbot and a Dominican friar at the same time? Finally I spoke, as respectfully as possible.

"Your Holiness, a plan like that would never work!"

We talked for a while longer. Finally the Pope raised his hand in a fatherly blessing. "I see no reason why your vows should be set aside," he said kindly. "You are really in earnest about your vocation. Go in peace, my son. From now on no one will interfere with your Dominican life."

In the autumn of that same year, I was ordered to accompany Father John, the Master General, on another trip to Paris. There were some business matters here which needed attention and I was to act as Father John's secretary. But we had not been long in Paris when there came some surprising news.

"I'll be leaving soon for Cologne, Brother Thomas,"

said the Master General. "You're to come with me. We've decided to let you attend classes under Father Albert."

I was very much thrilled. Father Albert of Cologne was one of the greatest scholars of the day. People came from all over Europe to study under this famous Dominican friar. At once I promised myself that the Order would never regret all the trouble I had caused it. With God's help, I would pray and study and work as I had never done before.

It was January of 1246 when I finally reached the great German city and enrolled in the classes taught by Father Albert. I made several friends in Cologne and soon found that the time I had spent as a prisoner at Monte San Giovanni had not been wasted. In those weary months in my tower I had been able to memorize many books, including the greater part of the Bible.

This was an immense help in my studies, although I never mentioned the fact to anyone. I realized God had given me an unusual memory. But why let my friends know about it? Their praise might have made me proud. Indeed, I was so quiet in class that many of the students thought I was stupid. Some of them even gave me a nickname—"The Dumb Ox of Sicily."

There were three reasons for this. First, I had been born in the southern part of Italy, not far from the island of Sicily. Next, I was big and strong for my age. Lastly, I was not known for having a quick tongue. I was a slow and solemn youth, people said. "The Dumb Ox of Sicily" was an excellent nickname.

I did not like being called a dumb ox, although no

one ever guessed it. Even Father Albert was inclined to believe me dull, for I had never told him about having the gift of a quick mind, or of having memorized most of the Bible. Nor had I ever said that many times I could have answered the questions that puzzled my fellow students. No, I remained silent and offered up the little sacrifice for my sins. There would be time enough later to be considered clever by my friends—if this really was God's Will.

One day, to amuse myself, I decided to write a paper on a certain problem in theology. It was a hard problem, and I spent a good deal of time in coming to a solution. Then I lost the paper. Probably it blew away or I absently placed it in some book. Anyway, it was discovered by no less a person than Father Albert. He promptly called me to the little cell where he spent so much time in reading and study.

As I opened the door he was looking at my paper in sheer amazement.

"Brother Thomas, did *you* write *this?*"

I looked carefully at the paper he handed me.

It was the one I had lost a few days before. "Yes, Father Albert. I wrote it."

"Why did you choose such a difficult problem?"

"I wanted to see if I could solve a really hard problem, Father."

My teacher looked me up and down. His eyes were suddenly very kind. "My son, you've been fooling us all the time," he said. "You're no dumb ox. I could not have written a better paper than this myself, and I am thirty-two years older than you."

I felt a little foolish. My desire to remain humble and unknown was a secret no longer. I felt even worse when I learned my teacher intended the whole school to know I was not stupid.

"I want you to take part in a debate," Father Albert told me. "If you can think and write as well as this paper seems to indicate, you should be able to speak pretty well, too."

Having promised obedience to my superiors, there was nothing for me to do but to take part in the next debate. The whole school came to hear it, students and teachers alike. I was given a subject to discuss. After I had finished, those who did not agree with me were allowed to argue their case. It was really the first time I had taken a leading role in a debate. Thanks be to God, things went very well for me. I— the slow, solemn youth from Rocca Secca—was able to prove all my points.

Father Albert was delighted. When I finished speaking, he rose to his feet and faced the whole assembly of teachers and students.

"We have called this boy a dumb ox," he said. "Some day his bellowing of God's Truth will be heard around the world!"

From this day on, no one teased me about being stupid. Father Albert even arranged that I should move out of my cell and take the one next to his. His books were at my disposal whenever I wished, and often he took me with him on his walks, so that we could talk together about God, about Heaven, about things in which both of us were interested.

CHAPTER FIVE

I GO TO PARIS

M Y STAY at Cologne was not very long—only six months. Then the superiors of the Order decided that Father Albert should go to Paris to study for the Doctor's degree. Since I still had a great deal of work to do before I could be ordained a priest, I was to go with him and attend classes at the University.

Being Dominicans, with no money to spend on luxuries, Father Albert and I walked from Cologne to Paris—a distance of fifteen hundred miles. It was the second time I had made this trip on foot, the first being when I accompanied the Master General from Paris to Cologne.

It was a hard journey. We begged for food from kind souls we met, spent the nights by the roadside, or at a monastery, if we could find one. Eventually we arrived at our own convent of Saint James in Paris, tired and dusty, but eager to get ahead with our studies.

I liked Paris very much. It was full of interesting people who had come to study at the University—at that time the greatest center of learning in Europe. One of my best friends in Paris was a young man named Brother Bonaventure. He was a student for the priesthood, too. But he was not a Dominican. He belonged to the Franciscan Order, and wore a brown habit with a cord about his waist and sandals on his bare feet. Often he would tell me of the man who had founded his great religious family—Saint Francis of Assisi.

"As a child I was sickly, Brother Thomas. No one thought I would ever be strong enough to do a good day's work. But one day Father Francis came and put his hands in blessing upon my head. Immediately I was cured of my poor health. I remember being full of joy at the miracle and hearing the Saint cry out in his sweet voice: *'O Bona Ventura!'*"

My friend then explained that *"Bona Ventura"* means "Good Luck," and that after Saint Francis had spoken these words, the boy who formerly had been so sick and helpless was known by them, although in a slightly changed form.

I liked this little story. It made me realize what a piece of good luck was mine that this Franciscan friar was my friend. He was four years older than I, and able to teach me a great deal about prayer, love and other virtues.

I remained in Paris for two years, at the end of which time I received the degree of Bachelor of Theology. The same honor was given Brother Bonaventure, too. Then Father Albert and I were ordered back to Cologne. I was to assist my former master in teaching at the Dominican school in that city. I also was to complete the last two years of study for the priesthood.

It was just about this time that I heard a piece of good news. My youngest brother, Rayner, had joined me in Saint Dominic's family. He was now a novice at our convent in Naples. Mother, it seems, was beginning to look more favorably upon the Dominicans. She had not raised any objection when Rayner sought to follow in my footsteps.

I was now twenty-three years old, and grateful for all the blessings God had showered upon me. Through His mercy, I had become a very successful teacher. Each week I gave lectures to great crowds of people on the Sacred Scriptures and philosophy. Hundreds of students were my friends, and many of these young people insisted I was of real help to them. They enjoyed my classes, they said. I seemed to have the gift of making even difficult things clear.

I was delighted at such words. And why not? Ever since I had been a small boy, I had lived with books. For years I had been interested in learning more about God, in helping others to do the same. Back at the Abbey school of Monte Cassino I had done my best to learn the answer to one question: *What is God?*

I know the good monks used to wonder what kind of lad I was, asking such a question, for it is one no human mind can answer completely. As a teacher, however, I did my best to answer it, and to help my students with other and less serious problems.

In the year 1250 came the wonderful day when I was ordained a priest by the Archbishop of Cologne. I was now twenty-five years old, and very happy in my work of teaching and study. Soon, I told myself, I might write some books that would help people understand the real meaning of life, why we have trouble when we want happiness, why there is such a thing as sin. But most of all, now that I was a priest at last, I would do the one thing that far surpassed all others: I would offer the Holy Sacrifice of the Altar.

The year 1250, that saw me a priest forever, was not without its sadness. The news reached Cologne that my brothers, Landulph and Raynald, had been killed in battle while fighting the cause of the Pope against the Emperor. At once I hastened to offer Mass for the repose of their souls. Long ago I had forgiven their harsh treatment of me. Now that I was a priest, the least I could do was to remember these brothers daily at God's holy altar—as well as Father, whose sole aim in life had been to see me Abbot of Monte Cassino.

My sisters were also in my thoughts during these first few weeks of my priesthood. Theodora was now married to the Count of San Severino. Marietta, however, had astonished everyone by becoming a Benedictine nun in Capua. She was the Abbess now, elected to this responsible post because of her holiness and sound judgment. As I thought about my sisters, about their many acts of kindness when I was a prisoner at home, I smiled. There was no doubt that now each had found her vocation, even as I had. Our roads were different ones, but someday, hopefully, they would have the same ending —at the throne of God in Paradise.

I taught four years at Cologne. Then, in the summer of 1252, word came that I was to return to Paris. Here I would present myself for the degree of Doctor of Theology. Although I was almost ten years under the required age, arrangements had been made for me to receive this high honor.

I was not anxious to take the Doctor's degree. In

Here was the finest book I knew.

spite of the many years I had spent at books, I felt I did not know enough to be considered a learned man. But I owed obedience to my superiors and once more started off on the long journey to Paris.

It was good to see my dear Franciscan friend again, now also a priest. Father Bonaventure was going to try for the Doctor's degree, too, and we spent much time discussing our work. Strangely enough, due to political troubles in Paris, we had to wait five years before presenting ourselves for examination. During this time I taught and preached a great deal, praying that my superiors would change their minds and tell me I need not try for the Doctor's degree. Alas, word came in October, 1257, that Father Bonaventure and I were to present ourselves before the examiners soon. Both of us would make a speech before the professors of the University of Paris. The topic would be a matter of choice.

On October 23, the night before the great day, deep sadness filled my soul. As yet I had prepared no speech. My whole being cried out against trying for the great honor.

"I haven't a thought in my head," I told myself hopelessly. "What am I going to do?"

I shut myself in my cell and knelt down to pray. For years I had done this whenever trouble came. My best writings, my most effective lectures, were always the result of kneeling humbly before God and asking His help. Indeed, the finest book I knew was the crucifix. Looking at it and thinking about its tremendous meaning, one could learn the most important things in the world.

As I knelt in prayer, a wonderful thing happened.

Saint Dominic, the founder of the Order I loved, appeared in my cell. He had been dead thirty-six years, yet God's mercy allowed him to come and bring me comfort.

"What is the matter?" he asked gently. "Why are you looking so sad?"

I stretched out my hands in the gesture of a beggar. "I have no speech ready for tomorrow, Father Dominic. My superiors expect me to do them credit at the University, but I'm afraid it will be a very poor show. In God's name, help me!"

Father Dominic smiled. "There is a good topic for your speech in the 103rd Psalm," he suggested. "Why not read it now? And take heart, my son. It is really God's Will that you obtain the Doctor's degree."

I was wonderfully encouraged by Saint Dominic's words. When morning came, I delivered at the University a talk which everyone praised. Later, in company with Father Bonaventure, I was presented with the degree of Doctor of Theology. Deep in my heart, though, as I accepted the great honor, I felt I did not deserve to be called wise. There were so many things I did not know, so many good acts I had left undone. What was any poor human mind when compared to the great, clear Mind of God?

In the years that followed my reception of the Doctor's degree, I did still more teaching and writing. The Pope asked me to take charge of a special group of scholars attached to his court. Wherever the Pope traveled, this school went with him. So it was that I had the chance to see Rome again, and Viterbo, Fondi, Orvieto, Perugia, Bologna and other Italian cities. In 1263 I even went to London, for the fortieth

General Chapter of the Order. Here I had the pleasure of meeting Father Albert of Cologne once more.

During these busy years of preaching, teaching and travel, God inspired me to do considerable writing, too. Sometimes I dictated to three or four persons at once—heavenly inspiration coming in floods. I composed explanations of the *Our Father*, the *Hail Mary*, the *Apostles' Creed*. I wrote about the Epistles of Saint Paul and about the errors in the Greek Church. I even wrote verses!

The books I wrote, while traveling from one European city to another, were not intended for children. My verses, though, became popular among people of all ages. Even today young people the world over know portions of my verses by heart. For these verses are hymns, and are heard at Benediction of the Most Blessed Sacrament. Here is part of one of these hymns, just as I wrote it over seven hundred years ago:

> *O Salutaris Hostia,*
> *Quae caeli pandis ostium!*
> *Bella premunt hostilia;*
> *Da robur fer auxilium.*
>
> *Uni trinoque Domino*
> *Sit sempiterna gloria:*
> *Qui vitam sine terinino*
> *Nobis donet in patria. Amen.*

Here is part of another:

> *Tantum ergo Sacramentum*
> *Veneremur cernui;*

Et antiquum documentum
Novo cedat ritui;
Praestet fides supplementum,
Sensuum defectui.

Genitori, Genitoque
Laus et jubilatio,
Salus, honor, virtus quoque
Sit et benedictio:
Procedenti ab utroque
Compar sit laudatio. Amen.

Why did I write my hymns in Latin? Because that was the language used by scholars in the thirteenth century—the period which was particularly my own. Today my books and verses have been translated into all the important languages. In English, the *O Salutaris* reads something like this:

O Saving Victim, op'ning wide
The gate of Heav'n to man below;
Our foes press on from ev'ry side;
Thine aid supply, Thy strength bestow.

To Thy great Name be endless praise,
Immortal Godhead, One in Three.
Oh, grant us endless length of days
In our true native land with Thee. Amen.

And the *Tantum Ergo* reads like this:

Down in adoration falling,
Lo! the sacred Host we hail;
Lo! o'er ancient forms departing,
Newer rites of grace prevail;

Faith for all defects supplying,
Where the feeble senses fail.

To the Everlasting Father,
And the Son who reigns on high,
With the Spirit Blest proceeding
Forth from Each eternally,
Be salvation, honor, blessing,
Might, and endless majesty.
Amen.

I wrote a number of other hymns in honor of the Blessed Sacrament, too. They are: *Lauda Sion, Sacris Solemniis* and *Adoro Te.* The last-named of these is often used as a prayer after Holy Communion and is to be found in most prayer books.

Chapter Six

I Go to Heaven

IT WAS Pope Urban IV who asked me to write my hymns on the Blessed Sacrament, as he was thinking of making a new feast in the Church. This was the Feast of Corpus Christi, and special prayers and hymns were needed. These would be used in the Mass and the Divine Office. The Pope also asked Father Bonaventure to try his hand at the same task. He would choose between us as to who did the better work.

Father Bonaventure was a real saint, as well as a great scholar. Perhaps I knew better than most people how much he loved God. There was no doubt his prayers and hymns for the new feast would be very fine. Nevertheless, since I had been ordered to do my best, I started to work.

One day my Franciscan friend came to see me. While he was in my cell, he happened to look at what I was writing on the Holy Eucharist. This was most unfortunate, for right away he said his own work was not worth showing to the Holy Father.

"You have written so well!" he cried. "The Holy Ghost has inspired you in a most wonderful way!"

"He's inspired you, too," I said quickly. "When may I see your work?"

Father Bonaventure shook his head. "I'll never let

One day my friend came to see me.

anyone see it. I'm going to burn all my worthless scribbling."

I was horrified at such words. "But you can't do that! You've spent so much time at the task!"

There were tears in my friend's eyes. "This work of yours will go down in history, Father Thomas. No one could do any better."

"Please let me see what you've done!" I begged. "Aren't we old friends? Won't you do me this one little favor?"

Father Bonaventure, good and humble soul that he was, would not listen. That very night he went back to his convent and burned the beautiful hymns and prayers he had written in honor of the Blessed Sacrament. As a result, the Pope had to be content with my work when the day for making a choice arrived. This was most unfortunate, for Father Bonaventure was known throughout the country as a very able man. On February 2, 1257 (a few months before we received the degree of Doctor of Theology), he had been elected Minister General of the Franciscan Order. There was no doubt that my friend could have produced some really beautiful prayers and hymns, if humility had not kept him from trying.

As the years passed, I continued to write and teach and travel. My greatest effort as a writer was the *Summa Theologica*, a collection of many volumes dealing with Catholic doctrine. I spent two years at Rome writing the first part. At Bologna I worked five years on the second part. The remainder (which I never really finished) was done at Naples. God was very good to me during these years of almost ceaseless activity. Once, as I knelt before a crucifix and thanked Him for His help in writing about the Blessed Sacrament, I heard His voice say very distinctly:

"You have written well of the Sacrament of My Body."

On another occasion, when I was at Salerno and writing about Christ's Passion and Resurrection, the crucifix spoke to me again:

"You have written well of Me, Thomas. What reward will you have?"

What could I say? I was overcome at still another miracle. With tears in my eyes I looked up at the crucifix:

"I want only You, O Lord!" I murmured. "Nothing else."

Presently I was called to Bologna to give some classes to the students there. My Dominican brethren greeted me warmly and made me feel very much at home in their convent. But one morning, while I was taking a walk in the garden, a young lay Brother hurried toward me and said I was to accompany him on a shopping trip.

"Father Prior told me to take as my companion the first friar I met," he said. "Will you get ready, please?"

It was easy to see that the good Brother did not know who I was, or that I had work to do on some lectures.

"Of course I'll come," I said. (I, too, was subject to the Prior.) "What do you want me to do?"

"You can help carry home the vegetables," said the Brother. "I'm going to get some at the market."

We started out briskly on our trip, but very soon I found myself growing tired. My companion was

a much younger man, and had the habit of walking fast. For years I had been used to little activity save reading or teaching. As a result, I made a poor showing at hustling over the cobbled streets of Bologna. And I was not much good at carrying packages, either. They made me tired in no time.

"What's the matter?" the lay Brother kept asking. "You're terribly slow. Don't you know we have to be back by dinner time?"

"I'm sorry, Brother. I guess I'm not accustomed to walking."

"It's the best kind of exercise, Father. You need a lot of it if you want to keep in good condition." And off he started again, his habit billowing out behind him like a sail, while I struggled with the packages and tried not to think of my aching feet.

Finally, as we were nearing the end of our mar' ing, I saw some priests and students whom I well. Of course they were surprised to see r ing along with my arms full of packages.

"Father Thomas! What are you doing cried.

I explained that I was helping the l the marketing—at least, I was tr' At once they started to question scold him for being so thought' priest to come shopping with

"Don't you know this is F they asked. "The profess'

The poor lay Brother he had heard about had never suspecte found strolling in the

"Oh, dear!" he cried, remembering how he had scolded me for not keeping up with him. "What will Father Prior say? What will the other friars say? Oh, Father Thomas! Please forgive me!" And he knelt down at my feet, his face a deep crimson and tears in his eyes.

The poor boy! I told him it was quite all right and not to worry anymore. There was nothing wrong about carrying vegetables through the streets. It was too bad if a Doctor from the University of Paris could not be useful in other ways than teaching and writing. Besides, the Father Prior had told him to take as his companion the first friar he met. I had been the first friar. Therefore we both had earned God's blessing by being obedient to the will of our superior.

On December 6, 1273, while I was saying Mass at the Dominican convent in Naples, God granted me a vision. For a moment I caught a glimpse of Heaven and the marvelous happiness of the blessed. From now on I found it hard to concentrate on any work. All the sermons I had preached, the books I had written, seemed useless as straw. There was no happiness on earth, no matter how great, that could equal the happiness God has in store for His friends.

"You haven't finished the *Summa Theologica*," my confessor, Father Reginald, one day. "Isn't it time you did some more work, Father?"

I shook my head. "My labors are over," I said quietly. "I shall never write or preach again. Death will come within a few months."

Father Reginald was sorely distressed at such a thought for a moment, then decided I needed rest. A visit with my sister Theodora, now

Countess of San Severino, would be the very thing.
He himself would accompany me there.

I tried to argue a little, then fell silent. How could
I explain that one glimpse of Heaven had killed all
desire for remaining longer in the world? That now
my one great hope was to go home to God?

Father Reginald and I set out for Theodora's castle around Christmas time. On the way I told him
secrets I had never before shared with anyone. I told
him of the cord about my waist, the cord two angels
had brought me over thirty years ago. I told him that
Marietta, the little sister who had become a Benedictine Abbess, who had died some years ago, had
appeared to me to say she was in Heaven. My two
brothers, Landulph and Raynald, were there, too.
The latter had informed me that soon I would join
them.

Father Reginald listened attentively to what I had
to say, but his heart was sad. He didn't want me to
die. I was only forty-eight years old, and the *Summa
Theologica* had yet to be completed.

"Maybe we should send word to the Franciscans,"
he murmured.

I smiled. Father Reginald was thinking of my good
friend, Father Bonaventure. A few months ago he
had been made a Cardinal by Pope Gregory X. He
certainly would wish to see me before I died.

"The Cardinal's a very busy man," I said. "Let's not
bother him just now with unimportant things."

When we reached Theodora's castle, my sister could
not control her anxiety. "You look so tired, Thomas!
Oh, dear! Why have you worked so hard?"

I smiled again. My young sister had grown into a

handsome woman, and it was plain to see she was very happy as the Count's wife.

"I am a little tired," I said. Then, because I felt it was the thing to do, I told Theodora that soon I was going to die.

"Thomas! You don't mean it!"

"I do mean it. And why look so distressed?"

"But you're not an old man yet!"

"No, but I think I have finished the work God gave me to do."

As the days passed, my sister continued to be amazed that I could face death so calmly. "You used to be so afraid of dying," she told me. "You'd run and hide whenever there was a thunderstorm. I remember that very well."

I remembered it, too. Until just a few weeks ago that old fear had persisted. The flash of lightning that had once struck the castle of Rocca Secca, killing our baby sister and leaving me badly shaken, had never faded from my mind. But I was not afraid of lightning now. Anything that could cause death, that could bring me to the Heaven of which I had been given one short glimpse, was most welcome.

"We should be sensible about death," I told Theodora as gently as I could. "It's only after we've died that real happiness begins. Did you ever think how much trouble our bodies cause us? They let us be only one place at a time. They grow hot and cold, hungry and tired. But in Heaven everything is so different. Dear Theodora, how eager I am to see that wonderful place!"

Theodora was understanding more and more about heaven and holiness. One day she asked me how to

become a saint. My reply was very brief. I said to her:
"Will it!" For I knew that God's grace is never lacking on the road to holiness. The problem is that we
do not make a firm, definite, absolute decision to be
a saint. If we did, we would certainly become saints
with God's grace.

In January of 1274 the Pope sent word that he
wished me to go to France to attend an important
meeting of priests and Bishops that was to be held in
the city of Lyons. So for a while I had to stop thinking of death. God leaves us on earth only until we
have finished the work He wishes us to do. Appar-
ently I had not yet finished mine.

We had not gone far on the road to Lyons when I
fell ill. Father Reginald, my ever faithful companion,
thought we should interrupt our journey for a visit
with my niece Frances, the Countess of Ceccano. We
did this, but after five days the feeling came to me
that it would be better to die on the road to Lyons, in
obedience to the Pope's wish that I be on my way to
the important meeting, than to breathe my last amid
comfort and luxury.

"Let's start," I begged Father Reginald. "I have
much more strength than you think."

Father Reginald loved me dearly. Any sign that my
health was improving brought new hope to his heart.
Yet he did not wish me to leave my niece's house.

"You're not strong enough to go to Lyons, Father
Thomas. The Pope would say the same thing if he
could see you."

I pleaded very earnestly. I even asked the Abbot
of the Cistercian Abbey of Fossa Nuova to try to
influence Father Reginald. He and his monks lived

a few miles distant and he was a visitor at my niece's house on the day I decided we must start for Lyons.

My arguments were finally successful. The Abbot ordered a mule to be brought so that I could continue the journey with less difficulty. Alas! We had gone but a short distance when I felt myself growing ill. We were seven miles from the Abbey. It was doubtful if my friends could get me there before death came.

I offered a quick prayer that I might not die on the road. Years ago I had learned to love the sons of Saint Benedict. Although I had never felt my vocation was to be their Abbot, I owed them a great debt of gratitude nonetheless. They had been my first teachers. Now, God willing, I would give up my soul in surroundings similar to Monte Cassino.

It was February 10. As the Abbot, his monks and Father Reginald joined in prayer for my intention, I felt a deep peace entering my heart. In some miraculous way I knew I was not to die on the road. God would give me sufficient strength to reach the Abbey.

As soon as we arrived at Fossa Nuova, I begged to be taken to the chapel. Here I thanked God for all His goodness and asked that He bless the students I had taught, my friends and relations. Then the Abbott had me carried to his own cell. Here nothing was lacking for my comfort. A fire was built on the hearth, so I would not be cold. Medicines were brought to ease my pain. The whole community remembered me at prayer.

For a while it seemed my health was improving. I knew better, however. My work for God was almost completed. "This is my rest forever and ever," I told

Father Reginald one day. "Here will I dwell, for I have chosen it."

Recognizing Psalm 131, the good friar wept. He did not want to lose me.

"Don't be sad," I told him. "We shall meet again in Paradise."

Then I closed my eyes. The words of a hymn I had written long ago, the *Adoro Te*, came into my mind. Slowly I began to recite the seven stanzas. Having finished, I breathed a great sigh. My days on earth were over at last!

CHAPTER SEVEN

I GO TO WORK

I WAS buried at the Cistercian Abbey of Fossa Nuova. After some years, however, my body was moved to the city of Toulouse, France, where it rests today. Many of my friends missed me when I went to Heaven, particularly my old teacher, Father Albert of Cologne. Yet God did not want too many tears shed. In His mercy, He allowed my poor body to have miraculous powers over sickness and disease. When invalids prayed beside it, they frequently rose up well. Even before I was buried, a blind monk at Fossa Nuova regained his sight by bending over and touching his eyes against mine.

It was all very wonderful to see God's power working in my body, to look down from Heaven and know that I still had work to do in bringing people to love my dear Saviour. But still more happiness was in store. This came to pass in 1880, when God put into the mind of Pope Leo XIII the idea of making me Patron of Catholic Schools. From then until this day my work has been to see that every Catholic boy and girl does well in school. I especially want Catholic boys and girls to learn their Faith well, for that is the most important thing they can know.

You who have read this story know quite a bit about me now. You have learned how eager I am

I am waiting to be your friend.

to help young people do well in school. But there is something else I want to do, too. I want to help boys and girls remain pure, in body and soul.

Remember when the angels brought me the cord with the fifteen little knots in it? They told me then that I should always have the gift of purity. Purity is one of the most exquisite gifts God can give a person. I want to help boys and girls to keep this gift. In fact, I think it would be a good idea if every young person in the United States belonged to my special society. This society is *The Angelic Warfare*.

Perhaps you never heard of *The Angelic Warfare*. Maybe not one boy or girl you know belongs to it. But let me tell you about this little group, whose aim is to help young people keep spotless the purity of their bodies and souls.

Older people may belong to it, too, but I am particularly anxious that all the boys and girls who have read this book become members as soon as they can.

My little society for young people had its beginning in the year 1649, at the University of Louvain, in Belgium. Since then it has spread all over the world, although it is not so well known in the United States and Canada as it might be. However, we can work at making it known, at seeing that every boy and girl who wants to grow up truly happy and successful belongs to it. God will certainly bless our efforts.

Is it hard to be a member of *The Angelic Warfare*? No. There are only five simple things to do:

1. Have one of my blessed medals.
2. Have your name put down on the register of

The Angelic Warfare by a priest who has the power to do so.

3. Wear my medal day and night.
4. Love Our Blessed Lady and ask me to help you do your work well.
5. Say the *Hail Mary* fifteen times every day in honor of the fifteen decades of the Rosary.

Is that very hard? Of course not. Any boy or girl can do these five simple things. And if you do them faithfully, you can be sure that I shall always pray for your work and your happiness—in school and elsewhere, and most of all, in the next life.

Perhaps you noticed that the first rule for membership in *The Angelic Warfare* is to have one of my medals. If you wish, you may wear a little cord with fifteen knots in it, something like the one the angels brought me and which is now kept at the Dominican church in Chieri, Italy. However, most boys and girls who belong to *The Angelic Warfare* wear my medal instead of the cord.

On one side of this medal there is a picture of Saint Dominic receiving the Holy Rosary from Our Blessed Lady On the other side two angels are shown putting the cord around my waist. I am listening to these blessed spirits say that God has promised I shall always remain pure in body and soul. This news has made me very happy. I am nineteen years old. I have decided I would rather die than become God's enemy through sin.

I think that you will like my medal. Your teacher or your pastor will tell you how to get one.

This is all I have to say. I hope you liked this book and that you will get all your friends to read it. Remember, I am Thomas Aquinas, the Patron of Catholic Schools. I am waiting to be your friend.

New York City
Feast of Saint Pius V
May 5, 1943

DECLARATION OF POPE LEO XIII

Brief Issued on August 4, 1880

"In virtue of Our supreme authority, for the glory of Almighty God and the honor of the Angelic Doctor, for the advancement of learning and the common welfare of human society, we declare the Angelic Doctor, St. Thomas Aquinas, Patron of all Universities, Academies, Colleges and Catholic Schools, and we desire that he should be venerated by all."

PRAYER TO SAINT THOMAS AQUINAS
BEFORE STUDY OR LECTURE

O BLESSED Thomas, Patron of Schools, obtain for us from God an invincible faith, a burning charity, a chaste life, and true knowledge, through Christ Our Lord. Amen.

PRAYER TO SAINT THOMAS AQUINAS
TO OBTAIN A SPECIAL FAVOR

D EAR Saint Thomas, gentlest of saints, you loved Jesus so tenderly and wrote so well of Him that He made you the glory of the Church and a shining star in the Order of St. Dominic. Encouraged by your kindness and charity, I beg you to obtain this favor that I now ask.

(State your request.)

Plead my cause with your beloved Jesus, so that I may serve Him faithfully in this life and enjoy Him forever in Heaven. Amen.

One Decade of the Rosary.

PRAYERS OF THE ANGELIC WARFARE

Recommended to Be Said Frequently
by the Members of the Society

PRAYER OF SAINT THOMAS AQUINAS

This prayer was said by St. Thomas as he lay prostrate before the cross which he had drawn upon the wall with the burning brand after repelling the last attack on his purity. Then the angels girded him with the cincture of perpetual chastity, a favor which his humility concealed until the approach of death, when he revealed to his confessor what had happened to him.

DEAREST Jesus! I know well that every perfect gift, and above all others that of chastity, depends upon the most powerful assistance of Thy Providence, and that without Thee a creature can do nothing. Therefore, I pray Thee to defend, with Thy grace, chastity and purity in my soul as well as in my body. And if I have ever received through my senses any impression that could stain my chastity and purity, do Thou, Who art the Supreme Lord of all my powers, take it from me, that I may with an immaculate heart advance in Thy love and service, offering myself chaste all the days of my life on the most pure altar of Thy Divinity. Amen.

Prayer for Purity

CHOSEN lily of innocence, purest St. Thomas! to thee who didst preserve ever fair thy baptismal robe; to thee who, being girded by two angels, didst become a true angel in the flesh! to thee do I pray to recommend me to Jesus, the Immaculate Lamb, and to Mary the Queen of Virgins, that I also, who seek to honor thee, may receive the gift of thy purity; that thus imitating thee upon the earth, I may one day be crowned with thee, O great guardian of my purity, amongst the angels in Paradise.

Our Father. Hail Mary. Glory be to the Father.

V. Pray for us, St. Thomas.
R. That we may be made worthy of the promises of Christ.

Let us pray.

O GOD, Who hast vouchsafed to defend with the blessed cincture of St. Thomas those who are engaged in the terrible conflict of chastity! grant to us Thy suppliants, by his help, happily to overcome in this warfare the terrible enemy of our body and soul, that being crowned with the lily of perpetual purity, we may deserve to receive from Thee, among the chaste bands of the angels, the palm of bliss. Through Christ our Lord. Amen.

When putting on the cord or medal say:

GIRD me, O Lord! with the cincture of purity, and by the merits of St. Thomas extinguish within me every evil desire, that I may remain continent and chaste until death. Amen.

ANOTHER PRAYER OF SAINT THOMAS

O MERCIFUL God, grant that I may eagerly desire, carefully search out, truthfully acknowledge, and ever perfectly fulfill all things which are pleasing to Thee, to the praise and glory of Thy Name. Amen.

PRAYER TO SAINT THOMAS AQUINAS PATRON OF CATHOLIC SCHOOLS

O ANGELIC Doctor, Saint Thomas, prince of theologians and model of philosophers, bright ornament of the Christian world and light of the Church; O heavenly patron of all Catholic schools, who didst learn wisdom without guile and dost communicate it without envy, intercede for us with the Son of God, Wisdom Itself, that the Spirit of Wisdom may descend upon us, and enable us to understand clearly that which thou hast taught, and fulfill it by imitating thy deeds; that we may become partakers of that doctrine and virtue which caused thee to shine like the sun on earth, and may at last rejoice with thee forever in their most sweet fruits in Heaven, together praising the Divine Wisdom for all eternity. Amen.

MARY FABYAN WINDEATT

Mary Fabyan Windeatt could well be called the "storyteller of the saints," for such indeed she was. And she had a singular talent for bringing out doctrinal truths in her stories, so that without even realizing it, young readers would see the Catholic catechism come to life in the lives of the saints. Mary Fabyan Windeatt wrote at least 21 books for children, plus the text of about 28 Catholic story coloring books. At one time there were over 175,000 copies of her books on the saints in circulation. She contributed a regular "Children's Page" to the monthly Dominican magazine, *The Torch*.

Miss Windeatt began her career of writing for the Catholic press around age 24. After graduating from San Diego State College in 1934, she had gone to New York looking for work in advertising. Not finding any, she sent a story to a Catholic magazine. It was accepted—and she continued to write. Eventually Miss Windeatt wrote for 33 magazines, contributing verse, articles, book reviews and short stories.

Having been born in 1910 in Regina, Saskatchewan, Canada, Mary Fabyan Windeatt received the Licentiate of Music degree from Mount Saint Vincent College in Halifax, Nova Scotia at age 17. With her family she moved to San Diego in that same year, 1927. In 1940 Miss Windeatt received an A.M. degree from Columbia University. Later, she lived with her mother near St. Meinrad's Abbey, St. Meinrad, Indiana. Mary Fabyan Windeatt died on November 20, 1979.

(Much of the above information is from *Catholic Authors: Contemporary Biographical Sketches 1930-1947*, ed. by Matthew Hoehn, O.S.B., B.L.S., St. Mary's Abbey, Newark, N.J., 1957.)

✠ SAINT BENEDICT ✝ PRESS

Saint Benedict Press, founded in 2006, is the parent company for a variety of imprints including TAN Books, Catholic Courses, Benedict Bibles, Benedict Books, and Labora Books. The company's name pays homage to the guiding influence of the Rule of Saint Benedict and the Benedictine monks of Belmont Abbey, North Carolina, just a short distance from the company's headquarters in Charlotte, NC.

Saint Benedict Press is now a multi-media company. Its mission is to publish and distribute products reflective of the Catholic intellectual tradition and to present these products in an attractive and accessible manner.

TAN·BOOKS

TAN Books was founded in 1967, in response to the rapid decline of faith and morals in society and the Church. Since its founding, TAN Books has been committed to the preservation and promotion of the spiritual, theological and liturgical traditions of the Catholic Church. In 2008, TAN Books was acquired by Saint Benedict Press. Since then, TAN has experienced positive growth and diversification while fulfilling its mission to a new generation of readers.

TAN Books publishes over 500 titles on Thomistic theology, traditional devotions, Church doctrine, history, lives of the saints, educational resources, and booklets.

For a free catalog from Saint Benedict Press
or TAN Books, visit us online at
saintbenedictpress.com • tanbooks.com
or call us toll-free at
(800) 437-5876